Past & Present

SEDALIA

OPPOSITE: Humboldt Hartenbach poses in the doorway of his cigar store at 120 East Second Street in the late 1890s. His business was flanked by the Post Office Exchange and a brick residence, both of which housed restaurants and bars. Hartenbach's store and the residence were torn down in 1916, when Best Laundry erected a $35,000 brick building on the site. The laundry building and two others were razed in 1964 to construct a parking lot. (Courtesy of Leslie Hale Collection.)

PAST & PRESENT

SEDALIA

Rebecca Carr Imhauser

This book is dedicated to my husband, Bill Imhauser. I'm thankful for our past and present—and looking forward to our future.

ISBN 978-1-4671-0405-0

Library of Congress Control Number: 2019947586

Published by Arcadia Publishing
Charleston, South Carolina

Printed in the United States of America

For all general information, please contact Arcadia Publishing:
Telephone 843-853-2070
Fax 843-853-0044
E-mail sales@arcadiapublishing.com
For customer service and orders:
Toll-Free 1-888-313-2665

Visit us on the Internet at www.arcadiapublishing.com

On the Front Cover: This photograph of Ohio Avenue in 1941, looking north from West Fifth Street, captures downtown just before the scene changed to support World War II. The Pettis County Courthouse lawn (right) became a scrap metal collection site, and City Light & Traction (near left, center) displayed used rubber in its showroom window. All of the landmark buildings remain. Most have been restored or are currently being renovated. (Top, courtesy of James Keck; bottom, author's collection.)

On the Back Cover: Sedalians remember this three-story building at 108 West Pacific Street as the longtime home of the J.A. Lamy Manufacturing Company. Completed in 1896, the building initially housed both the Mackey Shoe Company and Lamy's, as it was fondly known. The site at which Levis were manufactured for more than 50 years is now being transformed into retail, office, and residential space. The adjacent Clay and Heynen monument company was at this location from its founding in 1879 to 1948, when it moved to East Third Street. (Author's collection.)

Contents

ACKNOWLEDGMENTS

While my name appears on this book's cover, credit belongs to those who took the time to share their photographs and memories. The title of this series, Past and Present, also describes my countless visits with contributors. We reminisced about Sedalia's past and how those who came before us shaped our present.

A special thank-you to those who inspired me to begin recording history and through the years have provided ongoing encouragement: Mary McLaughlin, who introduced me to Arcadia Publishing, Anna Lee Bail, Millicent Hale, James Keck, and Jane Harris Yount. This book is a tribute to Leslie Hale, who wrote *Sedalia Missouri: 100 Years in Pictures* for Sedalia's centennial in 1960. He set the standard for pictorial histories of our town.

A happy coincidence enhanced this book: Tom Darrah shared selections from his collection of photographs and reference materials shortly before I found out I would begin this project. In addition, thank you to Pam Hunter, Arlene Silvey, and John Simmons, who provided access to invaluable archives or publications. I am grateful to the following who shared photographs, information, or professional expertise: Lewis P. Andrews III, Steve and Debbie Biermann, William B. Claycomb, Jack Clark, Linda Ellis, Amy Epple, David Esser, Joy Greer Fluty, Jerry and Kay Greer, Darrin Hartman, Scott Hunnell, Betty Bob Jones, James Jonson, Lee and Cheryl Keeting, Randy Kirby, Savannah Lynde, Selma Bloess Norton, Jack McMurdo, Byron and Judy Matson, Judy Greer Means, Tom and Becky Bingaman Munson, Robert M. Overstreet Jr., Dr. Mark Register, Paula Schupp, Aric Snyder, Garnetta Sullivan, Tom C. Taylor, Kevin Walker, Bob Walters, Ellen Weathers, Ralph Ludemann Wentworth, Sylvia Wilkinson, Bothwell Regional Health Center, First Baptist Church, Horace Mann Elementary School Archives, Inter-State Studio & Publishing Company, Michael Edwards Photography, Preuitt Insurance Services, Sedalia Area Chamber of Commerce, Sedalia Parks and Recreation, Sedalia Public Library, Sullivan Creative, Walker Photography, and WEB & Sons. Other images are courtesy of the author.

And, finally, thank you to my mother, Betty Wasson Singer, my writing partner and constant encourager.

Introduction

George R. Smith, Sedalia's founder, was ready for a fresh start when he approached the age of 30. The Kentucky resident had lost most of his inheritance during the financial depression of 1828 and 1829. Smith, his wife, Melita, and their daughters, Martha and Sarah, moved with their extended family to Missouri in 1833. They initially settled five miles northwest of what is now Sedalia.

Soon the Smiths relocated a few miles southeast to Georgetown, which became the first permanent Pettis County seat. While many considered Georgetown a promising city, Smith harbored concern about its future. He believed the city was destined for failure if it did not become a stop on the Pacific (later the Missouri Pacific) Railroad.

When Smith could not convince the people of Georgetown to invest in bringing the railroad to the city, he started his own town. He purchased 503 acres of prairieland four miles south of Georgetown and filed a plat on November 30, 1857. He named his new city after his younger daughter, Sarah, or "Sed," since he had already named a boat after his older daughter, Martha. Shortly after selecting the name Sedville, Smith visited Josiah Dent in St. Louis. Dent expressed interest in the new city but dismay at its name. "The 'ville' was decidedly objectionable, as it did not comport with the large and flourishing city of his dreams," Smith's daughter Martha wrote. Dent suggested the suffix "alia," in keeping with larger cities such as Philadelphia.

In 1859, Smith persuaded the Pacific Railroad to locate a depot on his land. The arrival of the first passenger train to Sedalia in 1861 was considered the beginning of the city, despite the fact that Sedalia had been officially founded a year before. Smith's image—and that of the new town—then began to change.

Sedalia was named the Pettis County seat in 1864, shortly before the Civil War ended. While the Civil War put Sedalia's growth on hold in some respects, it benefited the young city in others. According to I. Mac Demuth, troops stationed in Sedalia included "shrewd and observant men" who saw the new city's potential.

The end of the Civil War signaled the beginning of Sedalia's phenomenal growth. Several who had been stationed in Sedalia during the war returned to open businesses. The Missouri-Kansas & Texas (MK&T, or Katy) established shops in northeast Sedalia in 1870. In 1872, the Pacific Railroad established shops in East Sedalia. Railroads sustained the town for nearly a century. Sedalia was also a trailhead for cattle drives and host to flourishing stockyards.

The 1873 city directory applauded Sedalia's status: "It is now the chief agricultural, commercial, manufacturing, and railway centre—the chief metropolis of this portion of the state—containing over 8,000 of as enterprising, public spirited, energetic, and intelligent inhabitants as can be found in any city of its size in the United States."

Sedalia constructed a new $100,000 courthouse in 1885, and additional multistory brick buildings soon followed. By the end of the 1800s, towering brick buildings had replaced the city's decrepit wooden structures. Sedalia's downtown district was a center of commerce and culture.

Optimism prevailed as Sedalia closed the 19th century. Downtown's growth was grand, but Sedalia had higher aims—to be the capital of Missouri. The "Capital Removal Project," as Sedalia's initiative came to be known, spanned two decades. Despite the best efforts of leading Sedalians, a statewide vote in 1896 determined the Missouri capital would remain in Jefferson City. Sedalia lost its bid for the capital but gained the Missouri State Fair in 1899.

Sedalia grew immensely through the early part of the 20th century, largely due to railroad expansion. Its population increased from 15,231 to 21,444 between 1900 and 1920. The city entered the Roaring Twenties with a literal blaze, as fire destroyed its courthouse in 1920. A new courthouse was dedicated five years later.

Then came the Depression. Three out of four downtown banks closed within a three-month period from November 1931 to January 1932. Two officers of those banks committed suicide during the same period. *Life* magazine declared Sedalia the city second-hardest hit by the Great Depression in the entire United States.

Despite the hardship, Sedalians were united in their quest for better times. World War II continued to bring the city together through bond drives and support for soldiers stationed at the nearby Sedalia Army Air Field in Knob Noster, Missouri.

The postwar era brought the greatest changes to Sedalia since its founding. Businesses and services began moving outside the downtown core. Dr. A.J. Campbell Jr., a longtime Sedalia physician, succinctly summarized why he moved his office from downtown Sedalia to a new single-story structure near Bothwell Hospital. "Stairs, stairs, stairs," he said. His office, and that of his physician-father before him, had been located on the second floor of 312 South Ohio Avenue. Dr. Campbell noted that the stairs became an informal stress test for his patients. Patients' ability to climb the two flights of steps was a measure of their wellness.

Automobiles also brought wide-scale change to Sedalia. After World War II, automobile production increased along with the size of vehicles. The tail-finned behemoths of the 1950s were no match for downtown parking, which had been designed for horses and carriages. Historic downtown buildings were razed to provide parking lots.

The advance of automobiles collided with the decline of the railroad industry. Passenger trains had provided the main transportation to and from Sedalia for nearly a century. They arrived at Sedalia's two depots near downtown, which fueled the hotel and restaurant economy. That changed when automobiles began depositing passengers at motels, initially known as tourist cabins or camps, along Broadway Boulevard and South Limit Avenue. Broadway Boulevard, now US Highway 50, and South Limit Avenue, now US Highway 65, soon replaced downtown as Sedalia's main business corridors. Thompson Hills Shopping Center, which opened on West Highway 50 in 1964, and State Fair Shopping Center, which opened on South Limit Avenue in 1965, further drew people away from downtown.

The railroads' demise was offset by manufacturing and industry that swelled after World War II. Town & Country Shoes, Parkhurst Manufacturing, Rival Manufacturing, and the Pittsburgh Corning Corporation rose in Sedalia in the 1940s and 1950s. By the time the railroad shops had closed, other industries had moved to town to support its economic base. Alcan Cable, Duke Manufacturing, Kelsey-Hayes, Gardner-Denver, Waterloo Industries, and Payless Cashways became major employers. Industry continues to sustain Pettis County's economic base with companies such as Tyson Foods, Inter-State Studio and Publishing Company, Starline Brass, Sierra Bullets, ProEnergy, and Nucor.

Through the years, a myriad of people have helped transform George R. Smith's prairie town into a bustling hub of central Missouri. A new generation of visionaries is reviving culture and commerce downtown. Countless others are leaving their distinctive mark on the community. Smith envisioned a city that would provide opportunities for his family and those who came after them. His dream lives on through the people who continue to call Sedalia home.

CHAPTER 1

FOUNDATIONS

The establishment of Sedalia as the Pettis County seat in 1864 is one of many foundations from which the city grew. The county court met in a variety of locations until this $100,000 courthouse was completed on the present courthouse square in 1885. The crown jewel of the Queen City, this courthouse was destroyed by fire in 1920. (Courtesy of Mary McLaughlin.)

Many people caught their first glimpse of Sedalia from the Pacific depot. The two-story building at Pacific Street and North Osage Avenue was completed in 1886 and is pictured below in May 1950, the same month an extensive reconstruction began. Workers removed the second floor and renovated the exterior. The interior of the remaining ground floor was gutted, leaving a ranch-style building in keeping with the era's fascination with Western motifs. The depot now is a multimodal transportation center that includes Amtrak. (Below, courtesy of Leslie Hale Collection.)

The $40,000 Missouri-Kansas & Texas depot was erected in 1896 at East Third Street and Thompson Avenue. By 1988, the once-bustling station had been abandoned by the railroad and acquired by the Missouri Department of Natural Resources. A $3-million restoration and build-out began in 1998 and was completed in 2001. The Katy Depot Historic Site is a year-round visitor destination serving as Sedalia's welcome center and includes an exhibit gallery, gift shop, and event space.

In 1867, seven-year-old Sedalia used a childlike argument to construct a viaduct over the Pacific Railroad tracks at East Main Street and Washington Avenue: "Everyone else is doing it!" Civic leaders thought Sedalia needed an iron bridge because other towns were building them. The first viaduct was completed in 1868 and removed in 1872 for railroad improvements. Because it was accessible only by foot, the bridge was considered worthless. A new viaduct was built in 1911 to accommodate vehicle traffic.

The 1861 view below of the north side of the 100 block of East Main Street is one of the earliest known photographs of Sedalia. During this era, business owners built wooden sidewalks in front of their individual stores. This resulted in sidewalks of varying heights, with levels that abruptly changed between businesses. The original buildings no longer exist, nor do the dusty or muddy streets and uneven sidewalks. Phase I of downtown Sedalia's streetscape, which was dedicated in 2009, included this block. (Below, courtesy of Leslie Hale Collection.)

The Sedalia City Hall was completed in 1875, providing space for offices, the market house, the city jail, and an engine room. The police force is pictured below in front of the building in 1957. Proposals to replace the building were repeatedly defeated until voters approved a one-percent city sales tax in 1970. The city's new $750,000 municipal building, shown above, was dedicated in 1973 on the city hall site. (Below, courtesy of Jack Clark.)

Two lampposts at the northwest corner of West Third Street and Kentucky Avenue have illuminated the way to a variety of buildings and businesses through the years, including a residence, doctors' office, rooming house, and hair salons. The photograph above shows a sales office for Bryant Motors, constructed after the residence was torn down. A new police department headquarters was completed on the site in 2019. (Above, courtesy of Tom Darrah.)

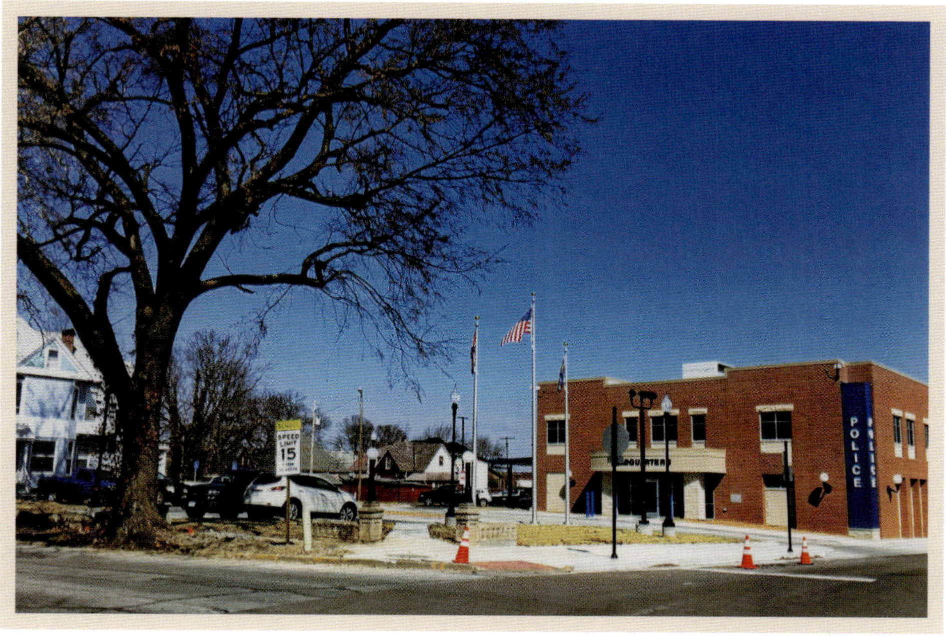

This standpipe rose from the middle of a major highway. Located at the intersection of Highway 50 and Engineer Avenue, it measured 15 by 125 feet and held nearly 6,000 cubic feet of water. The standpipe was constructed to increase water pressure for fighting fires and to provide a reserve for drought. Drivers heaved a collective sigh of relief when it was removed in 1920 after the installation of a pumping station. (Left, courtesy of Mary McLaughlin.)

For more than six decades, a 20- by 250-foot smokestack towered over Sedalia's electrical power plant at Ninth Street and Ingram Avenue. The photograph below shows the plant, which through the years included a cooling reservoir and power house. City Light and Traction, later Missouri Public Service, operated the power plant. The final plumes of smoke wafted from the smokestack in 1977. It was torn down in 1984 by the same company that had built it in 1923. (Below, courtesy of Sedalia Public Library.)

Dr. W.C. Overstreet is pictured below in front of his office at 106 West Fifth Street, along with his horse that pulled his buggy for house calls. The building was erected in 1913 with Dr. Overstreet's reception and consultation rooms on the ground floor and his living quarters and library upstairs. His nephew Robert Overstreet bought the building and operated Acme Cleaners there for 36 years until retiring in 1967. (Below, courtesy of Robert M. Overstreet Jr.)

Sedalia attorney John H. Bothwell provided the city $150,000 through his trust to establish a hospital and hotel. The Bothwell Memorial Hospital opened in 1930, a year after his death, near Ingram Avenue and Fourteenth Street. The original hospital, currently known as Bothwell Regional Health Center, has expanded numerous times through the years. The top of the original building above is visible near the center of the image below. Bothwell Regional Health Center now has multiple locations.

Sedalia experienced phenomenal growth in the late 1880s when the Sturges brothers posed for the photograph above in front of their lumber business at East Third Street and Massachusetts Avenue. Thomas J. Sturges (center) and Gould A. Sturges (right) owned Sturges Bros. Lumber until 1945, when Home Lumber bought the business. The left section of the building was home to Richard Olmstead's State Fair Livery in the early 1900s. (Above, courtesy of Leslie Hale Collection.)

Elaborate parades were among Sedalia's earliest forms of recreation and entertainment. The procession below, moving through the 100 block of West Main Street around 1899, is likely associated with a circus. Famous circus companies frequented Sedalia during this era, arriving on multiple train cars and setting up at Liberty Park. The photograph above shows the longtime location of Cash Hardware and the Maple Leaf Tea Room and Antique Mall (left) and Looie's Clothing, now Juanita's House Antiques (right).

Sedalia's municipal airport opened in 1944 on 906 acres six miles west of town. Air shows, such as seen below, were a popular attraction. Jack Funk leased the airport and offered flying lessons and plane rides for a penny per pound of each passenger's weight. When Sedalia's new municipal airport opened east of town in 1953, this land was returned to agricultural use. In 1989, Louis Rich began building a turkey processing plant that is now Tyson Foods, visible in the background above. (Below, courtesy of Jack McMurdo.)

The Missouri Farmers Association (MFA) grain elevator on Clinton Road is pictured above during construction in 1957. One of the most modern elevators in the area, it represented a $160,000 investment by about 1,700 MFA members. The elevator could process about 6,000 bushels per hour at top speed and had a storage capacity of 125,000 bushels. The grain elevator is now one element of MFA Agri Services, located near the former MK&T Railroad Shops, now Katy Park. (Above, courtesy of the Sedalia Public Library.)

Patriotism and service—firm foundations for Sedalia—are represented in the 1942 photograph above of a new American flag and pole being dedicated at Elks Lodge No. 125 at Kentucky Avenue and Fourth Street. Boy Scouts and Company F, 4th Missouri Infantry, are among those pictured during the ceremony. The Messerly Apartments (at center) were razed in 1969 for a parking lot. A new building (below, right) for Brown's Automotive Supply, now Boonslick Regional Library, replaced the large apartment building in 1947. (Above, courtesy of Leslie Hale Collection.)

Organized in 1871, Sedalia's Library Association initially occupied the second floor of 115 South Ohio Avenue. The Sedalia Public Library was founded in 1895 and was located in the basement of the Pettis County Courthouse. Andrew Carnegie awarded Sedalia a $50,000 grant in 1899 to construct the present library building at 311 West Third Street. Sedalia was the first city in Missouri to receive such a grant. The library was dedicated in 1901.

Home cooking is one of Sedalia's most heartwarming traditions. Leonard and Mattie Greer operated the White Swan Café on Engineer Avenue from 1939 to 1979. Mattie was known for her made-from-scratch chili, grilled tenderloins, hot toasted cheese sandwiches, burgers, and curly-Q fries. To the delight of students at nearby Washington Elementary School, the café had an entire wall of penny candy. Renowned artist Jesse Barnes, Mattie Greer's brother, painted the café's logo on the side of its truck as well as a commercially marketed painting of the café. (Below, courtesy of Jerry Greer and Judy Greer Means.)

CHAPTER 2

Downtown

Streetcar 102 awaits passengers at the Porter Block near Ohio Avenue and West Main Street in this early 1900s photograph. Today, its picture invites readers to board for a block-by-block overview of buildings along Ohio Avenue, moving south from Main Street, through the pages of this book. The streetcar will also make stops at landmark buildings on nearby streets. (Courtesy of Leslie Hale Collection.)

Union Savings Bank anchors the 100 block on the east side of Ohio Avenue, looking south, in the 1940s photograph above. Jeweler Charles Taylor erected the building to its right in 1871 to house three businesses. Taylor's building was razed in 1964 for construction of a drive-through bank facility. Dick's Barber Shop and the VFW Post 2591 are among the businesses shown below. (Above, courtesy of the City of Sedalia Archives.)

The Sedalia Drug Company was located at 124 South Ohio Avenue (below, left) in the late 1930s. It moved to the center building (122 South Ohio Avenue) in 1939. Owner Howard E. Robinson was associated with Sedalia pharmacies for more than four decades. The drugstore was known for its pharmacy, over-the-counter drugs, cosmetics, and sundries—and especially for the soda fountain and booths in the back. The Thrifty Dress Shop operated at 120 South Ohio Avenue (right) from 1937 to 1971. (Below, courtesy of James Jonson.)

Sarah Smith Cotton and Martha Smith, daughters of Sedalia founder George R. Smith, erected a three-story building at 209 South Ohio Avenue in 1893. The photograph below showcases its turret, carved stone faces, and curved and stained-glass windows. The upper floors were removed in 1970 as part of a modernization for the Singer Sewing Center store. The building now houses Stone Laser Imaging.

In 1885, William Ilgenfritz erected the Ilgenfritz Block at Third Street and Ohio Avenue. Meuschke Dry Goods occupies the first floor in the photograph at right, with professional offices upstairs. Later longtime businesses included Chasnoff's and J.C. Penney department stores. A matching addition, shown at right below, was erected for the F.W. Woolworth Company in 1915. The Commerce Building apartments now occupy the building following a $7-million renovation completed in 2011.

The view of South Ohio Avenue above between West Third and West Fourth Streets dates to 1898. At that time, the 300 block of South Ohio was bounded by a bank at each end. The Sedalia National Bank is at right above, and the Sedalia Trust Company is at left. Both closed in 1932 during the Great Depression. The Sedalia National Bank became Crown Drug Store in 1936 and now is Swords' Family Pharmacy (below, right).

In 1882, brothers-in-law William Messerly and Henry Meuschke opened their dry goods store in a new building at 310 South Ohio Avenue. The building was later combined with three others to its north. Longtime occupants of the expanded retail space included the S.S. Kresge Company and Jupiter Discount Store. The Pro-Velo Cycle Sport store now occupies the building, with Becca's Framing to its north. (Below, courtesy of Ralph Ludemann Wentworth.)

The O.&W. Drug Store at 312 South Ohio Avenue is pictured below in the early 1890s when operated by David M. Overstreet and Seymour Brady Williams. Seymour Williams is standing in the doorway at left in a long-sleeved white shirt. The office of Dr. W.C. Overstreet was located above the drugstore, and Charles Townsley Jewelry was in the building at left. The photograph above shows buildings erected by Charles and Merritt Yeater in 1914. (Below, courtesy of Sylvia Wilkinson.)

The Hotel Bothwell opened at Ohio Avenue and East Fourth Street in 1927. It featured more than 100 guest rooms, a coffee shop, a barbershop, a beauty shop, and retail stores. The $410,000 hotel soon became a stopping place for the distinguished and famous, including Pres. Harry S. Truman, Bette Davis, Clint Eastwood, and Sally Rand. The Furnell Companies restored the hotel and reopened it in 1999. It now is part of Choice Hotel's Ascend Hotel Collection. (Right, courtesy of Bothwell Regional Health Center.)

The Pettis County Courthouse caught fire in 1920 while tinners were repairing its dome. Flames rapidly consumed the structure, and its burned-out hulk remained the centerpiece of downtown Sedalia for nearly three and a half years. The county court appointed a committee to consider rebuilding the old structure or constructing a new courthouse. The committee decided in favor of a new building, shown above during construction in 1924. The present Pettis County Courthouse was dedicated in 1925. (Above, courtesy of Darrin Hartman.)

The 1940 photograph at left shows 404 South Ohio Avenue during an extensive remodel for Star Drug. The project included reconstructing the facade, removing the vault from the former People's Bank, and adding a balcony that seated more than 100 people. The building was the center storefront of the Latour Block, constructed by renowned photographer William Latour in 1879. The facade was returned to a historic look in 2002. The Two-Bit Barber opened at the site in 2018. (Left, courtesy of James Keck.)

John Colaflower completed a five-story, $50,000 building in 1893 for F.E. Hoffman at 500 South Ohio Avenue, now the location of Fitter's 5th Street Pub. E.G. Cassidy constructed the building pictured to its left in 1892. In 1932, during the Great Depression, upper floors were removed from both structures when they were remodeled for chain grocery stores. The New Lona Theatre (later Liberty Theater) was built on the site of the stable visible at right below.

Four generations of the McLaughlin family owned a furniture store and funeral chapel operating side-by-side for 129 years. George and John McLaughlin erected this building at 515 South Ohio Avenue in 1890. After the furniture store closed in 2009, Mary McLaughlin donated the building to State Fair Community College. Harvey and Carolyn Miller purchased the furniture store building in 2016 for Nostalgia Vintage Apparel and Marketplace. Jason and Bethany Weiker now own the McLaughlin Funeral Chapel. (Above, courtesy of Mary McLaughlin.)

W.L. Porter's $15,000 building at 518–520 South Ohio Avenue opened in 1900 with W.H. Ramsey's Racket Store on the street level. John M. Hill's business college soon moved upstairs. In 1904, Porter built a matching storefront at 516 South Ohio Avenue. The Poole & Creber Market, Firestone Tire, and Wade's Bake Shop occupied the space when the photograph above was taken. Later businesses included Beverly's Snack Shop and Demand Shoes. The building has been home to the State Fair Floral Company since 1988. (Above, courtesy of James Keck.)

In 1921, a $25,000 service station was constructed for the Producer's Oil Company at the corner of Ohio Avenue and Seventh Street. In 1962, the Milton Oil Company completed the present building, initially occupied by the Sedalia branch of the Internal Revenue Service and the American Automobile Association. The Schlobohm-Preuitt Insurance Agency (now Preuitt Insurance Services), moved to 622 South Ohio Avenue in 1985. The Preuitt Insurance team is pictured above. (Above, courtesy of Preuitt Insurance Services; below, courtesy of Ellen Weathers.)

In 1905, Christian Streng and Henry Kroencke commissioned this $12,000 building at 700–704 South Ohio Avenue. Streng operated his bakery in the center and southern storefronts until his retirement in 1919. The Shaw Music Company moved to 702 South Ohio Avenue in 1938, and Cecil's Cyclery moved to 700 South Ohio Avenue in 1952. Those businesses anchored the block for more than half a century. Today, the Streng and Cecil portions of the building have been restored and are occupied by New to You and Craft Beer Cellar.

Above, bunting and pennants herald the Missouri State Fair at the south entrance to downtown Sedalia around 1913. A century later, Phase IIIa of the streetscape provides a new entrance to downtown Sedalia on Ohio Avenue near Broadway Boulevard. The 47- by 27-foot gateway, resembling a railroad trestle to honor Sedalia's railroad heritage, was erected in 2015. Colorful murals now adorn Chelsea's Antiques and House of Vacuums in the 700 block of Ohio Avenue. (Above, courtesy of Aric Snyder and Inter-State Studio; below, courtesy of Bob Walters.)

By the 1870s, brick buildings had replaced many of Sedalia's original frame structures. The photograph of the 100 block of East Main Street above shows Archias' Seed Store building at left, constructed in 1879. The adjoining building was erected for Citizens National Bank in 1872. Fire destroyed the three-story Sedalia Candy Company building at right in 1948, when it was occupied by the Shryack-Wright Grocery Company. The streetcar tracks at center were removed during the Great Depression.

When Henry Kroencke died in 1958 at the age of 92, his obituary stated that he held the record as the oldest car salesman in the United States. He became an agent for Dort automobiles in 1915, and was selling Chevrolets in the 1950s when he was in his 80s. Kroencke's Dort dealership and his department store at 210–214 West Second Street are pictured below. In addition to automobiles, Kroencke is remembered for founding Kroencke's Concert Band, the forerunner of the Sedalia Concert Band, which continues to perform in Sedalia. (Below, courtesy of Leslie Hale Collection.)

James Glass erected a three-story building at the corner of Third Street and Lamine Avenue (below, left) in 1892 for his wholesale liquor business. This became the west end of the Dorn-Cloney Laundry, which operated at the site from 1907 to 1971. Fire destroyed the buildings a year after the laundry closed. The Cromwell Crest apartments were built on the site in 2018. (Below, courtesy of the Sedalia Public Library.)

J.T. and C.G. Heard erected a three-story building at the corner of Ohio Avenue and Third Street in 1871 (left). The next year, Joseph and Frank Sicher opened a bakery on the ground floor and an elegant hotel upstairs. In 1878, the Sichers expanded the hotel on East Third Street (right). The hotel later was known as the Elks, Antlers, and Royal. Classic Jewelry now occupies the bakery space, and the Septagon Construction Company is located in the East Third Street hotel addition. (Above, courtesy of the Sedalia Public Library.)

After Dr. E.A. Wood completed his new building at 120 West Fifth Street in 1916, he and four other medical professionals moved to the second floor. The City Market grocery occupies the street-level space in the 1937 photograph above. During World War II, it became the USO headquarters. Sedalia Industrial Loan & Investment and E.W. Thompson Edsel-Rambler sales were located at the site in the 1950s. Truman Title now occupies the building. (Above, courtesy of the Sedalia Public Library.)

In 1906, Porter Real Estate moved into its new two-story building at 112 West Fourth Street. It is pictured below in 1947, along with the adjoining *Sedalia Democrat* building. The newspaper moved from this location in 1967 to its new plant on Massachusetts Avenue, and the building at 110 West Fourth Street was razed. US Bank is located at left above, and the Trust Building is at right in both photographs. The Porter building now houses professional service firms. (Below, courtesy of James Keck.)

Montgomery Ward moved its tire and farm store to the northeast corner of Fourth Street and Kentucky Avenue in 1960. E.W. Thompson had erected this building in 1948 for his farm implement business. Thompson, Mike O'Connor, and Montgomery Ward had businesses in this building at the same time they occupied the site across the street, on the southeast corner of Fourth Street and Kentucky Avenue, pictured on the next page. A bread outlet was in this building after Ward's closed in 1986. The Pettis County Ambulance District now occupies the corner. (Below, courtesy of Tom Darrah.)

In 1949, E.W. Thompson expanded his automobile dealership building to span the entire block of Fourth Street between Osage and Kentucky Avenues. This building at the southeast corner of Fourth Street and Kentucky Avenue housed Mike O'Connor's automotive business from 1953 until 1960. Montgomery Ward occupied the building from 1960 until closing in 1986; it now is home to the ABC Advertising Agency. The First United Methodist Church is pictured at left above. After fire destroyed the building in 2016, the congregation erected a gazebo and prayer garden on the site.

The Mid-Continental Petroleum Company erected the cream-and-red stucco service station above at 620 South Osage Avenue in 1930. Dr. Floyd Lively replaced the station with the present building for his optometry practice in 1956. Founder of the Eye Clinic of Sedalia, Dr. Lively retired from practice in 1986. He and his wife, Geraldine "Gerry," died two days apart in 2013. Mi Pueblito is now located at the site. (Above, courtesy of Leslie Hale Collection.)

The Barney Bertman Oil Company built a new filling station in 1928 at the southeast corner of West Main Street and Missouri Avenue, then the new Highway 65. Richard Esser opened a drive-in liquor store at the site in 1960. Below, Standard Oil crowns are visible on the front pillar, and aluminum window frames have been installed on the first bay. Later remodels enclosed the first bay and added a wine cellar. (Both, courtesy of David Esser.)

Henry Fisher and Leslie McMullin operated the Grand Cleaners at the southeast corner of West Main Street and Grand Avenue in the early 1950s. The building housed a service station in the 1930s with a free-standing restaurant and garage buildings to its south. It was later extended to the south and was occupied by a bar and restaurants for several decades. (Below, courtesy of Lee and Cheryl Keeting.)

CHAPTER 3

Schools and Churches

Education and worship have been priorities for Sedalia since its founding. Broadway School was completed in 1868 at 301 West Broadway Boulevard. The building most Sedalians remember replaced the original school (pictured) in 1904. Broadway School operated until 1962; the building was razed in 1968. Third National Bank erected its new main bank on the site in 1980. (Courtesy of Leslie Hale Collection.)

Sarah Smith Cotton, daughter of Sedalia founder George R. Smith, donated land for the Smith-Cotton High School. The $400,000 building was constructed in 1925 directly behind the Smith home on East Broadway Boulevard. The photograph above dates to 1931, shortly after the Smiths' house was torn down, as evidenced by the mounds of soil in the foreground. The school became Smith-Cotton Junior High School when the $30-million Smith-Cotton High School opened in 2010 on the south end of Sedalia. (Above, courtesy of Sedalia Public Library; below, courtesy of Scott Hunnell.)

Lincoln High School was erected in 1927 and renamed in honor of Christopher Columbus Hubbard in 1943. Professor Hubbard was the school's principal from 1906 until his death in 1947. After closing as an educational center in 1980, Hubbard High School was renovated as the Lincoln Hubbard Apartments in 2009. The apartment complex honors the history of the school by displaying historic photographs and memorabilia.

The Sacred Heart School and parish were established in 1882, with classes held in the church building. Sacred Heart School, shown below, was built on West Third Street in 1907. The school added a gymnasium in 1948 and classrooms and a cafeteria to the east in 1956 (above, right). The photograph above also shows a three-story addition and a gymnasium that were completed in 2005 and 2009 to the left of the original building. (Above, courtesy of Scott Hunnell.)

Built in 1911, Horace Mann Elementary School was originally called the new Southwest School. The name was changed in 1912. The original building (above, right) cost $30,000 and housed eight classrooms. Enrollment swelled from 234 students in 1948 to 453 in 1955, leading to expansions on the west side (left in both photographs) in 1950 and east side (below, right) in 1954. The third addition to the school, on the southeast corner of the original building, was made in 1984. (Below, courtesy of Horace Mann Elementary School Archives.)

Whittier Elementary School, pictured above in 1959, was located at 915 East Sixteenth Street. The school and Striped College closed in 1990, when they were replaced by the new Parkview Elementary School. Whittier's gymnasium-auditorium (below, left) continues to be used by Whittier High School. The elementary school building was razed in 1991, and a new building for the Pettis County Health Center (below, right) opened on its site in 1993. (Above, courtesy of the City of Sedalia.)

Washington Elementary School opened at East Sixth Street and South Engineer Avenue in 1924. The new school was built immediately east of Summit School and replaced that building, which dated to 1884. Some of the fixtures from Summit School were salvaged to reduce the cost of building Washington. A multipurpose addition, constructed in 1988, appears at right above.

Calvary Episcopal Church is the oldest continuously occupied church building in Pettis County. Organized in 1865, the congregation met in various locations for more than two decades. The present native gray stone church building was completed in 1886 at the northeast corner of Broadway Boulevard and South Ohio Avenue. The rectory is pictured to the right of the church. Built in 1893, the rectory is now a private home.

When Sacred Heart Church was under construction in 1893, the *Sedalia Weekly Democrat* observed, "The glittering spires of the church have held aloft their golden crosses in the sunlight until they could be seen from far beyond the limits of the city." This statement about the landmark church, located at Third Street and Moniteau Avenue, remains true today.

Above, Flora Mackey Andrews (left), Sarah Mackey (right), and Lewis Peter Andrews Jr. (front) pose in front of their home at Fourth Street and Washington Avenue around 1910. St. Patrick's Catholic Church (right) and the Sisters of St. Joseph convent (left) are in the background. St. Patrick's School was built on the site of the home and convent in 1924 and operated until 1969. The building became a community center before being razed in 2019. The site is being returned to its residential roots, with apartments being constructed. (Above, courtesy of Lewis P. Andrews III.)

The Central Presbyterian Church built a $12,000 sanctuary at the corner of East Fifth Street and Lamine Avenue, adjacent to its former sanctuary (below, left), in 1911. The Presbyterian church united with another congregation in 1929, and the Salvation Army moved to the building. The Salvation Army remained until 1993, when it relocated to a new community center at 1200 East Broadway Boulevard. The Bethel Family Church now worships at this location.

The photograph below of First Baptist Church, located in the 600 block of South Lamine Avenue, shows two historic sanctuaries. One built in 1924 is at left. This sanctuary was built on the site of its 1893 predecessor, a portion of which remains near the center. The photograph above shows a new sanctuary, constructed in 1976 (right), and the Christian Life Center (left), dedicated in 1998. (Below, courtesy of First Baptist Church.)

CHAPTER 4

Homes and Highways

In 1867, A.D. Jaynes laid out a 120-foot-wide street named Broadway Boulevard. There, he and three other wealthy, influential Sedalians pledged in 1870 to build homes costing $8,000 to $10,000 each. Their neighbors later included Congressman John T. Heard, who built the home pictured here in 1906. Through the years, Broadway Boulevard transitioned into Highway 50. Some of Sedalia's homes and businesses along Broadway Boulevard and South Limit Avenue are featured on the following pages.

The Maples, A.D. Jaynes's home (above), was completed in 1871 at Broadway Boulevard and Ohio Avenue. Presidents Rutherford B. Hayes and Ulysses S. Grant were among its distinguished guests. The home became Maywood Hospital and was razed in 1932. Garst's (later Eddie's) Drive-In and a gasoline station were built on the site, as well as the Sedalia Armory, named for Maj. Gen. John C. "Jack" McLaughlin III. In 2016, Maple Square, shown below with the armory at left, opened to provide physical therapy and urgent care.

In 1876, D.H. Smith built one of Broadway Boulevard's four original mansions at the intersection of Ohio Avenue. He later constructed nearly identical brick homes for his daughters to the west, which are shown at left in both photographs. A filling station was built on the site of Smith's home in 1932. In 1974, a new building was erected for Winchell's Donut House. It became a Subway sandwich shop in 2011. (Below, courtesy of Betty Bob Jones.)

Numerous stately homes east and west of Sedalia's central business district remain on Broadway Boulevard/Highway 50. Dr. William E. Bess, his wife, Rosie, and dog Scotty are pictured below in 1942 in front of their home at 700 West Broadway Boulevard. Dr. Bess practiced medicine in Sedalia for more than 50 years. Kevin Walker, who purchased the house in 2003, re-created the past photograph. (Below, courtesy of Bothwell Regional Health Center; above, courtesy of Walker Photography.)

When Joseph Imhauser built this $15,000 residence in 1896, the *Sedalia Democrat* described it as "a palatial home." The three-story house at 705 West Sixth Street featured 20 rooms, six fireplaces, six stained-glass windows, and a third-story billiard and "general resort room." Henry W. Harris, president of Sedalia's Third National Bank, purchased the home in 1898, and it remained in the Harris family until 1977. Current owners Byron and Judy Matson purchased the home in 2005 and have expanded its heritage of historic preservation. (Above, courtesy of Jane Harris Yount.)

When businesses began moving from downtown in the early 1950s, the Kroger grocery store was among the first. The supermarket relocated in 1954 from its longtime home at 602 South Ohio Avenue to a new shopping center called Broadway Plaza at Broadway Boulevard and South Warren Avenue. The 12,000-square-foot store is pictured above during its grand opening. Harbor Freight opened in the former Kroger building in 2017.

Wayne Richardson opened a forerunner of today's convenience stores at 2401 West Broadway Boulevard in 1938. At its grand opening, the *Sedalia Democrat* reported customers could drive in for car service, have lunch delivered to their automobile, and receive curbside deliveries from the grocery store. In 1956, Richardson opened a Coast-to-Coast hardware store in the building. The structure was razed in 1984 for construction of a Shoney's restaurant. After a brief stint as a Big Boy restaurant in 1999, Denny's opened in 2000.

The Fairview Cabin Camp, at Highway 50 and State Fair Boulevard, offered lodging, dancing, food, alcohol, and gasoline as far back as the 1930s. An IGA Foodliner replaced the cabins and restaurant in 1962. Ralph Huff and Leo McNeal purchased the grocery store in 1964 and renamed it McNuff Market. In 1988, it became Bob's AF Super, owned by Bob and Elle Wasson. Later, it became a Dollar General. The shopping center expanded through the years and was renamed Fairview Shopping Center in 1991. (Below, courtesy of Tom Darrah.)

The 50 Hi-Way Motel, at 2700 West Broadway Boulevard, was one of numerous motels constructed along Sedalia's thoroughfares in the 1950s. By 1960, it boasted 20 units with a television and telephone in every room, plus automatic gas heaters, bathtubs, and showers. The motel was converted to retail and office space known as Cambridge Square in 1977. In 2017, the buildings were razed for construction of a strip mall called The Crossing.

Hush puppies are still available at 3500 West Broadway Boulevard, now as a seafood accompaniment rather than footwear. Town & Country Shoes, which opened in Sedalia in 1943, erected this building as its outlet store in 1991. It later became known as the Hush Puppies Factory Direct store, as the Wolverine footwear company had purchased Town & Country in 1982. LeMaire's Cajun Catfish & Seafood House moved from South Highway 65 to the former shoe outlet building in 2010. (Above, courtesy of Tom Darrah.)

The Katz Drug Company was one of the first stores to open in Thompson Hills Shopping Center. E.W. Thompson broke ground for the $4-million center in 1964 on his former cattle ranch west of Sedalia. The 28,500-square-foot Katz store was readily identified by its sign topped by a towering cat head. Katz Drug became Skaggs in 1972 and Osco in 1985. Big Lots opened in the building in 2005.

This corner of Highway 50 and Main Street was once occupied by Miller's, a restaurant known for its steaks and chicken, as shown below. Steak in the form of burgers is now served near that location at Steak 'n Shake, built in 2014. Philip Pfeiffer purchased 70 acres north of the site in 1947 for his retail and wholesale business associated with Pfeiffer's Flower Shop, which operated in Sedalia from 1875 to 2005. Extensive retail development began in the area with the opening of Menard's in 2010.

For 60 years, the Wheel-Inn drive-in anchored this corner of Highways 50 and 65. In 1947, Lyman and Ruth Keuper opened the landmark, which gained national recognition for its distinctive architecture as well as signature Guber burgers. When intersection expansion made it necessary to raze the drive-in in 2007, a Verizon Wireless store was built on the site. The Keupers constructed the brick building to the left of the Wheel-Inn in 1957; it is now occupied by Robert Rollings Architects. (Above, courtesy of Anna Lee Bail.)

W.E. Bingaman built State Fair Shopping Center on 14 acres at the corner of South Limit Avenue and West Sixteenth Street. Its first phase opened in 1965, including Bing's Supermarket. Wood's Supermarket opened at the site in 2017. The landmark smokestack sign remains from Dr. Julian Cannaday's greenhouses for the State Fair Floral Company, which occupied the land prior to the shopping center. (Above, courtesy of Tom Munson, WEB & Sons.)

Cash Hardware was State Fair Shopping Center's first tenant, in its northeast corner. That section of the shopping center is pictured below when it was being prepared for a new tenant. Note Sirloin Stockade's big cow, visible at left over the roofline, promoting the steakhouse, which opened in 1973. Sherwin-Williams moved from 512 South Ohio Avenue to the former Cash Hardware site in 1976. (Below, courtesy of Tom Munson, WEB & Sons.)

In October 1977, E.W. Thompson sold six acres at 3201 West Broadway Boulevard to Wal-Mart. One year later, in October 1978, the same page of the *Sedalia Democrat* reported both the passing of Thompson and the grand opening of Wal-Mart. A new Wal-Mart Supercenter opened directly behind the former Wal-Mart Discount Store in 1993. The $6.5-million building was more than twice the size of its predecessor. (Below, courtesy of Tom Darrah.)

CHAPTER 5

ENTERTAINMENT AND RECREATION

Entertainment and recreation have been a significant part of Sedalia since the town's earliest days. George R. Smith began erecting an opera house (right, topped by a flag) on the south side of West Main Street in 1868. The marble-front building cost $25,000 and seated 400 on its main floor and 400 in its gallery. While fire destroyed Smith's opera house in 1888, the legacy of entertainment and culture originated by Sedalia's founder lives on.

The image above appeared on the program guide for Hitchy Koo, the New Lona Theatre's first road show, in October 1920. The new $200,000 theater was on West Fifth Street, with its entrance on South Ohio Avenue. The New Lona later became a movie theater and was renamed Liberty Theater. After the Liberty closed, the building became a warehouse for Beatrice Foods. Community efforts began to convert the building back to a theater in 1983. It now houses the Liberty Center Association for the Arts. (Above, courtesy of Selma Bloess Norton.)

The 200 block of South Ohio Avenue offered entertainment in its early years through a pool hall known as the Smoke House, which was located where the Uptown Theater was constructed in 1936. The Uptown Theater (right) is in the process of restoration as a live theater event center. The C.W. Flower Company, one of Sedalia's leading department stores, was located north of the Uptown from 1907 to 1990. The Venue, LLC, an event center, opened in the building in 2018. (Below, courtesy of the Sedalia Public Library.)

The line for movie-goers often stretched from the Fox Theater, which opened in 1940 on East Fifth Street, around South Ohio Avenue. Besides showing motion pictures, the theater hosted war bond drives, fashion shows, school functions, fundraisers, and concerts until it closed in 1987. Furnell Companies transformed this area in 2009 into the Fox Theater Event Center and three-story Landmark Building.

The sketch above, published in 1880, shows the proposed Sicher's Driving Park. Frank and Joseph Sicher paid $10,000 for the site of the former Pettis County fairgrounds and spent $30,000 improving the 50-acre tract, adding mile and half-mile tracks, a 5,000-seat grandstand, and five-acre lake. The park also had an elegant hotel with a dining room that seated 500. The photograph below shows the same location, now Liberty Park. The convention hall is near the center. (Below, courtesy of Sedalia Parks and Recreation, Michael Edwards Photography.)

Liberty Park's convention hall was completed in 1912, the result of a $60,000 bond issue passed by voters in 1911. The early photograph above showcases architectural features that have been removed from the original $27,000 structure. The porch was razed in 1971 after vandals knocked down one of its walls. Bricks salvaged from the porch were used as part of a $150,000 facelift. (Above, courtesy of Leslie Hale Collection.)

Pond, lake, or lagoon—regardless of its name, this body of water at Liberty Park has been a Sedalia tradition for more than a century. Ice-skating in the early 1900s has given way to fishing in recent years, when the lagoon is regularly stocked by the Missouri Department of Conservation. The 1928 photograph below shows park visitors near the bridge and pagoda, both popular locations for weddings and other special events.

The Liberty Park pool shown below opened in May 1950 along with a new pool at Hubbard Park. The Liberty Park pool measured 140 by 70 feet and had a capacity of 500 swimmers. Admission was 15¢ for children and 39¢ for adults. A new $1.7-million pool, shown above, opened in 1997.

The photograph above shows the main gate for the Missouri State Fair in 1929. At that time, admission was 50¢ for adults and 25¢ for children. In 1939, James Keens was given 30 days to complete a new Art Deco gate, shown below. Keens and his crew were paid $2,000 for their efforts. (Above, courtesy of the Sedalia Pubic Library; below, courtesy of Randy Kirby.)

Originally known as the Livestock Pavilion, the Coliseum at the Missouri State Fairgrounds was built in 1906 and restored in 2001. It is one of several buildings on the fairgrounds designed by Sedalia architect Thomas Bast. While generally used for livestock events and horse shows, the Coliseum also serves as a public meeting place. Four US presidents have spoken there: William Taft, Harry Truman, Ronald Reagan, and George W. Bush.

Before the days of funnel cakes and kettle corn, Anna Kaler operated a diner at the fairgrounds. The photograph below from 1931 shows her second building. Her first was destroyed in 1916 by a fire believed to have been set by tramps. Ironically, Anna's husband, Frank, was assistant chief of the Sedalia Fire Department at the time. The Missouri Beef House now occupies the building. (Below, courtesy of Sedalia Public Library.)